In Hospital

Daphne Butler

SIMON & SCHUSTER

LONDON • SYDNEY • NEW YORK • TOKYO • SINGAPORE • TORONTO

Notes for parents and teachers
This book has a theme that threads its way through the topic. It does not aim to deal with the topic comprehensively; rather it aims to provoke thought and discussion. Each page heading makes a simple statement about the illustration which is then amplified and questioned by the text. Material in this book is particularly relevant to the following sections of the National Curriculum:

English: AT2 levels 1–3
Science: AT1 levels 1–3, AT2 levels 1–2, AT3 level 3
Technology: levels 1–3 (systems and environment)

△ Remember to warn children that medicine should only be taken as prescribed, and that it can be dangerous if used carelessly.

TAKE ONE has been researched and compiled by Simon & Schuster Young Books. We are very grateful for the support and guidance provided by our advisory panel of professional educationalists in the course of the production.

Advisory panel:
Colin Pidgeon, Headteacher
Wheatfields Junior School, St Albans
Deirdre Walker, Deputy headteacher
Wheatfields Junior School, St Albans
Judith Clarke, Headteacher
Grove Infants School, Harpenden

British Library Cataloguing in Publication Data
Butler, Daphne, *1945–*
   In hospital.
   1. Great Britain. Hospitals
   I. Title   II. Series
   362.11

ISBN 0–7500–0290–5

Series editor: Daphne Butler
Design: M&M Design Partnership
Photographs: ZEFA
except pages 10, 15, 20, 24.
Telegraph Colour Library
page 13TR, 14, *cover* Camilla Jessel

First published in Great Britain in 1990
by Simon & Schuster Young Books

Simon & Schuster Young Books
Simon & Schuster Ltd
Wolsey House, Wolsey Road
Hemel Hempstead, Herts HP2 4SS

© 1990 Simon & Schuster Young Books

All rights reserved

Printed and bound in Great Britain
by BPCC Paulton Books Ltd

Contents

Visiting time	6–7
At the clinic	8–9
Hurt in an accident	10–11
Staying in	12–13
Seeing the doctors	14–15
Taking your temperature	16–17
Medicine	18–19
Having an injection	20–21
Looking at pictures	22–23
Your blood	24–25
Having an operation	26–27
Going home	28–29
Index	30–31

6

Visiting time

Have you ever been to hospital?
Can you remember sights, sounds
and smells?

Perhaps you went to see a new baby
or to visit a friend.   Why else do
people need to go to hospital?

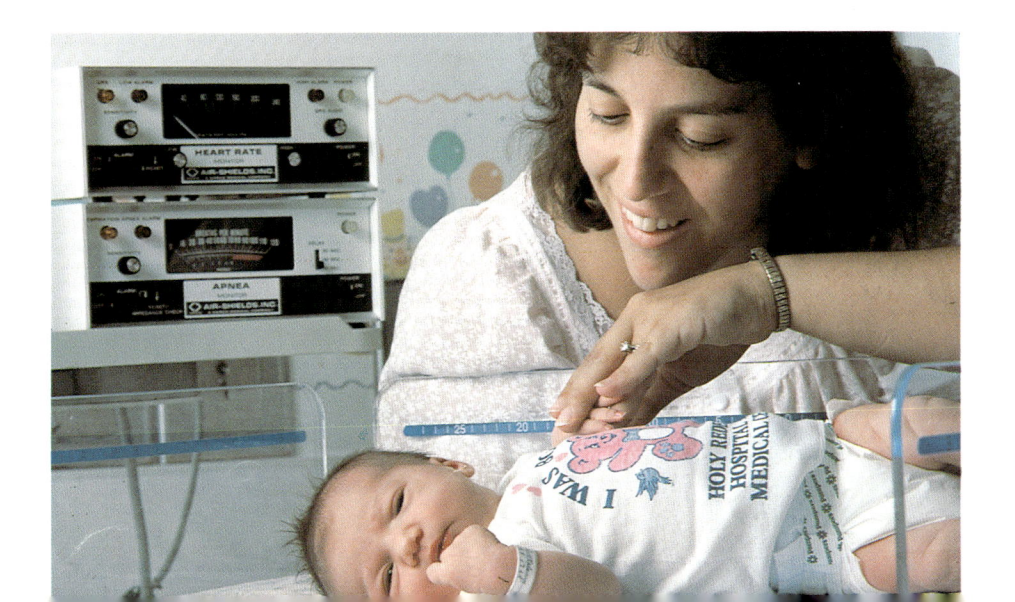

At the clinic

Have you been to a clinic
at the hospital?

Clinics are held for all kinds
of reasons, such as broken bones,
or difficulties with ears or eyes.

You have an appointment and see
the doctor.   Then you go home again.

St. Andrew's C.E. First & Middle School

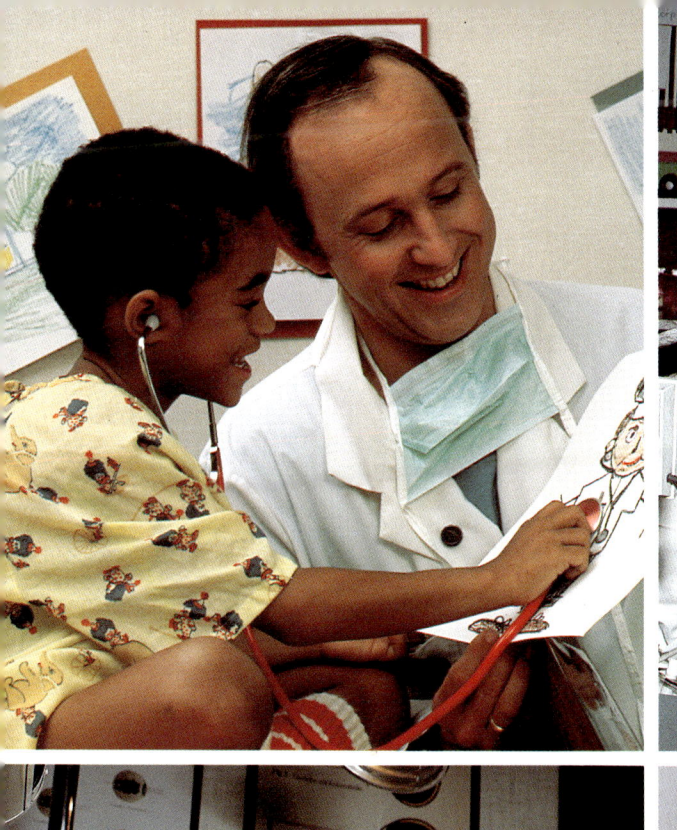

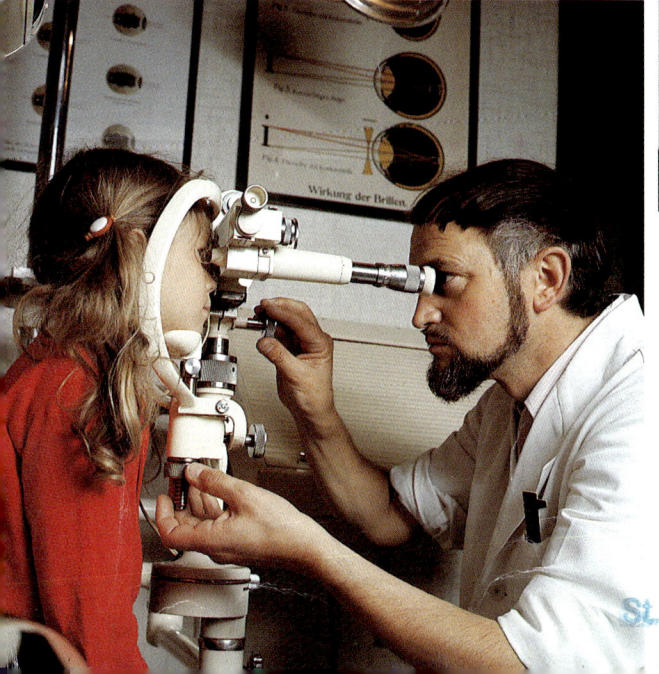

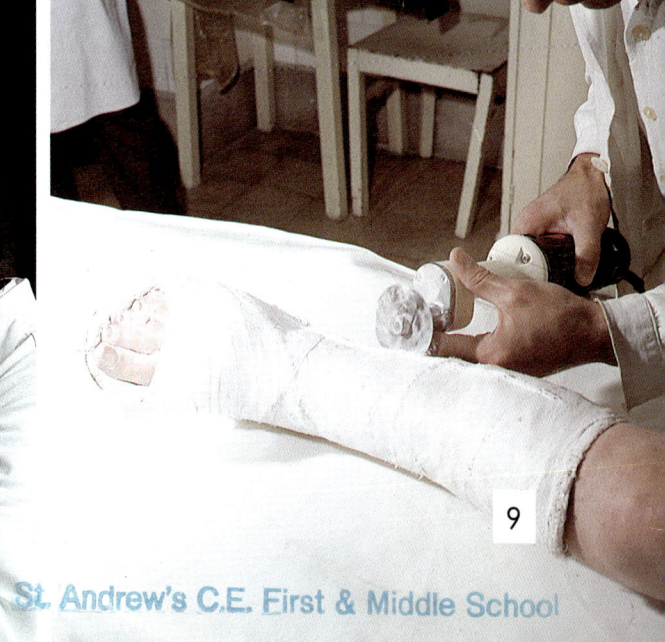

9

10

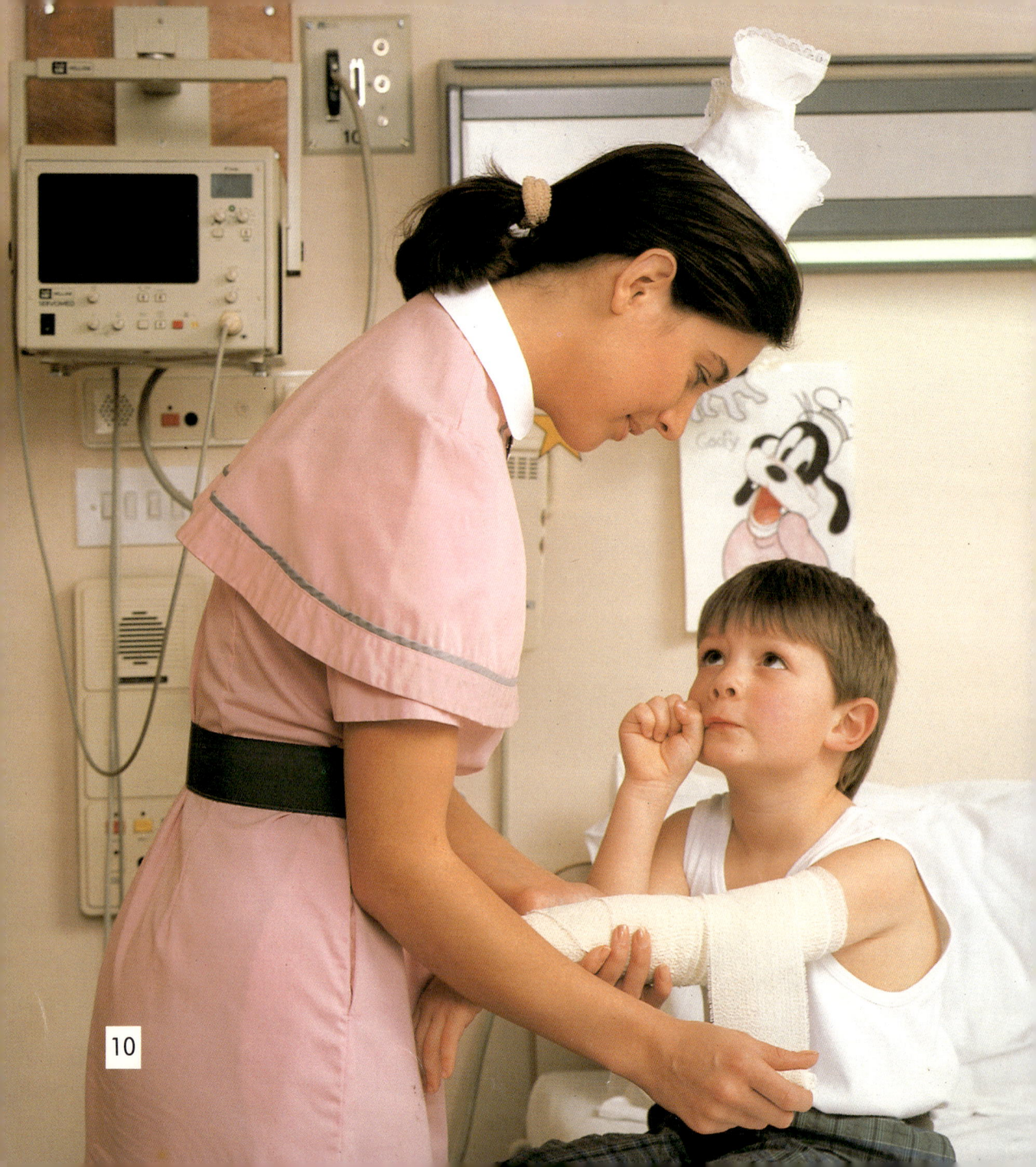

Hurt in an accident

Sometimes people need help quickly, in an emergency.

They might have a bad cut that needs stitching, or a twisted ankle that needs bandaging.

Most people go home after seeing the doctor, but some have to stay in hospital.

Staying in

When you stay in hospital
the nurses give you a bed in
a big room called a ward.

Imagine staying overnight in hospital.
What do you think it is like?

Sometimes mum or dad can stay too.

13

Seeing the doctors

The doctors come to see you every day. They check to see how you are and decide how they can make you well again.

The nurses look after you and follow the doctors' instructions.

15

St. Andrew's C.E. First & Middle School

Taking your temperature

The nurses take your temperature and your pulse, and record them on a chart.

The chart helps the doctors decide how well you are.

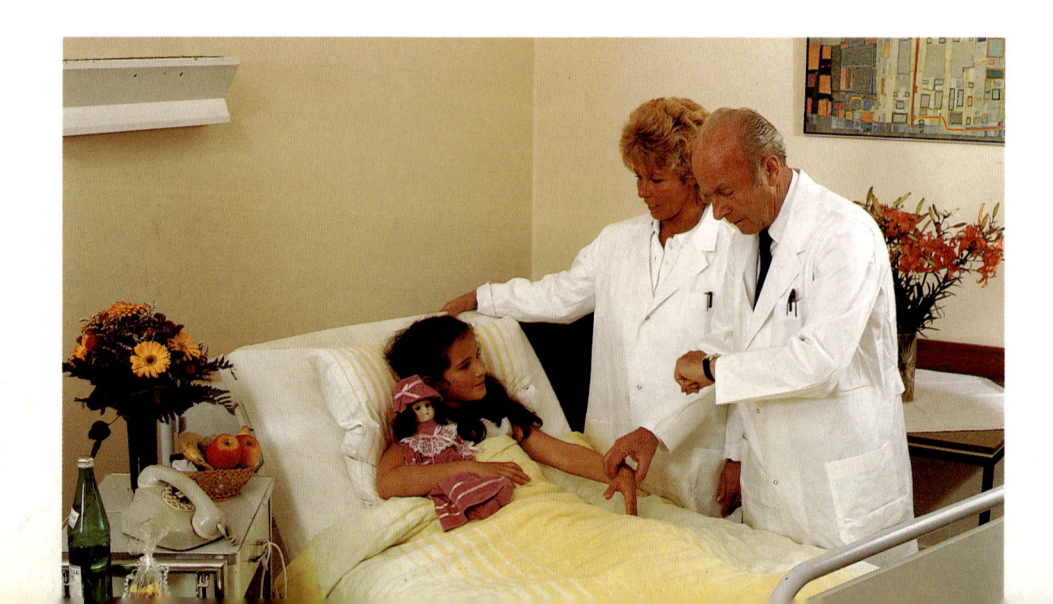

17

18

Medicine

The nurses give you the medicine prescribed by the doctors.
They get it from the medicine cupboard.

The nurses check very carefully to make sure they get the right medicine for you.

Having an injection

Some medicines need to go straight into your body.   The nurses do this by giving you injections.

They know just how to put the needle in without hurting you.

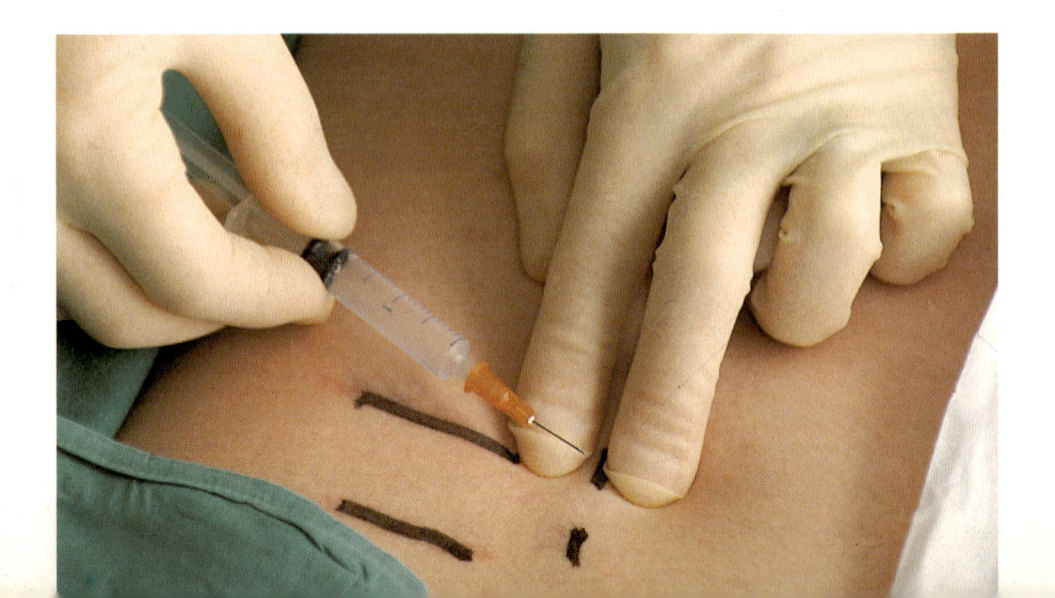

21

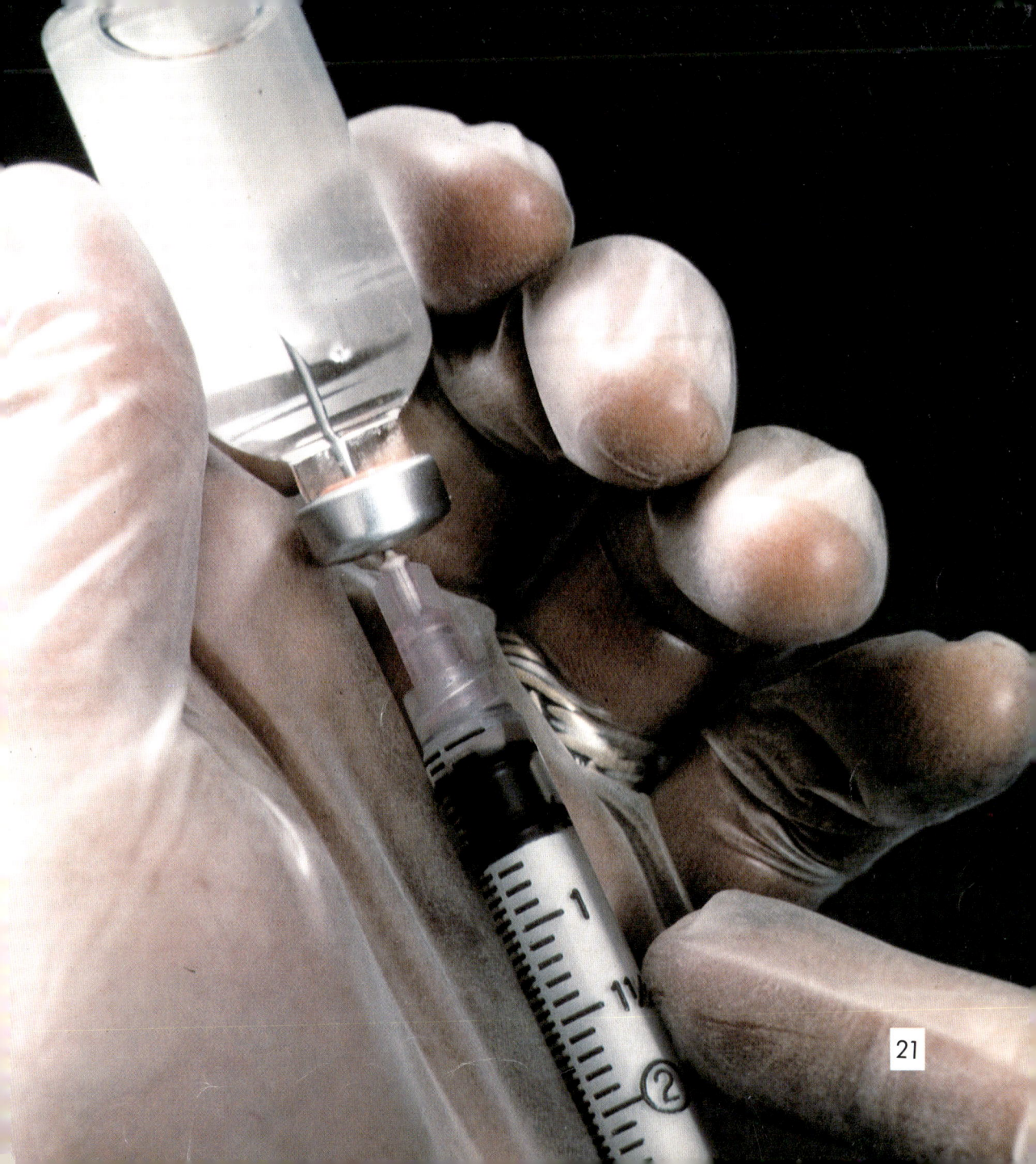

22

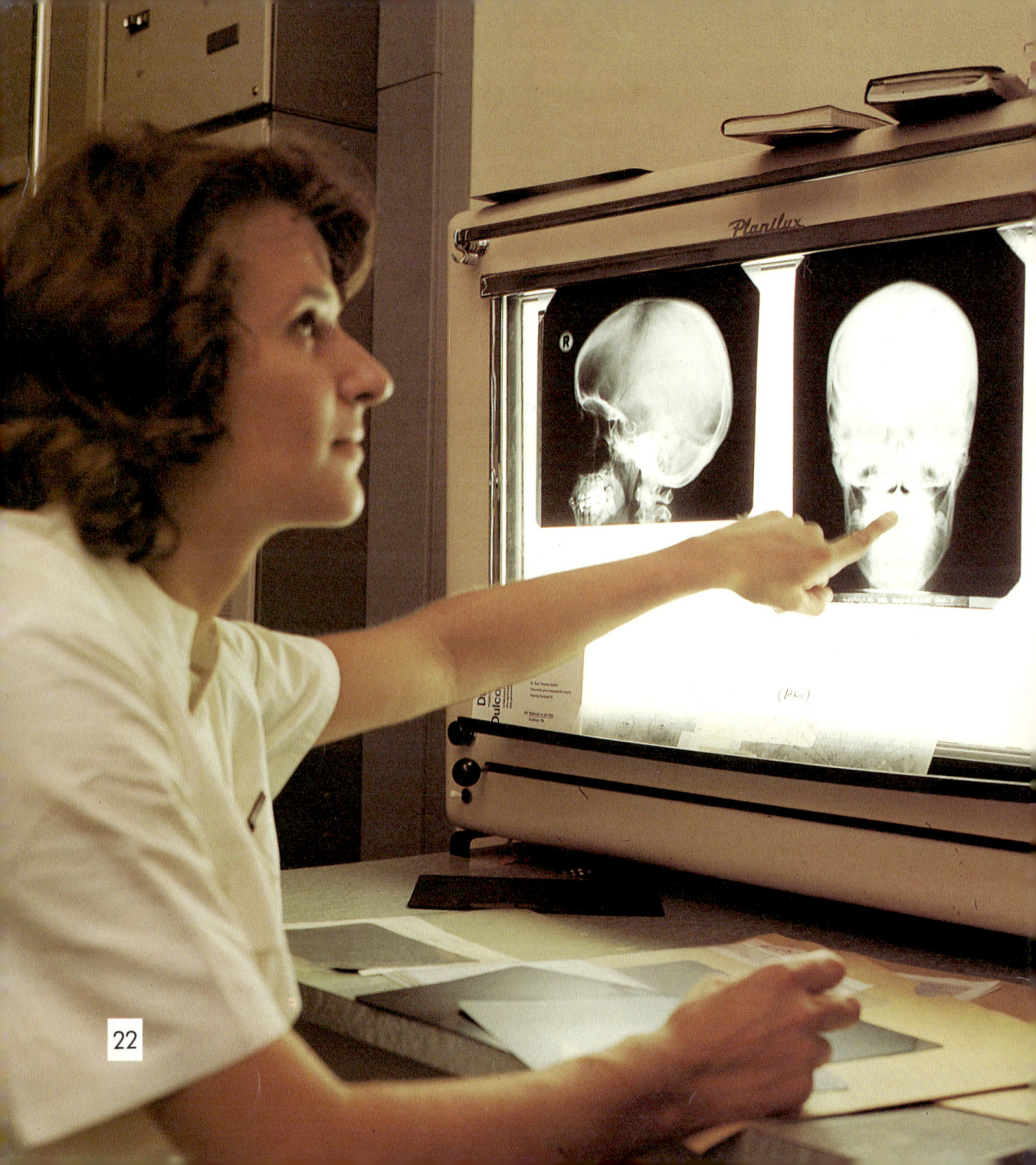

Looking at pictures

X-rays are photographs that show bones as white shapes. Other photographs give coloured pictures and show the flesh too.

The doctors use photographs to help make you better.

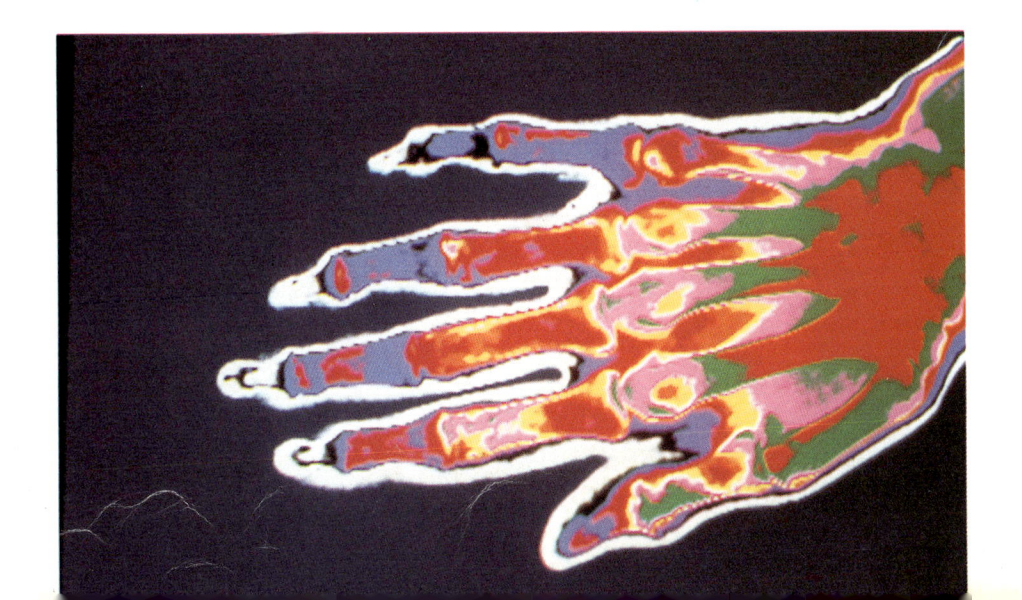

24

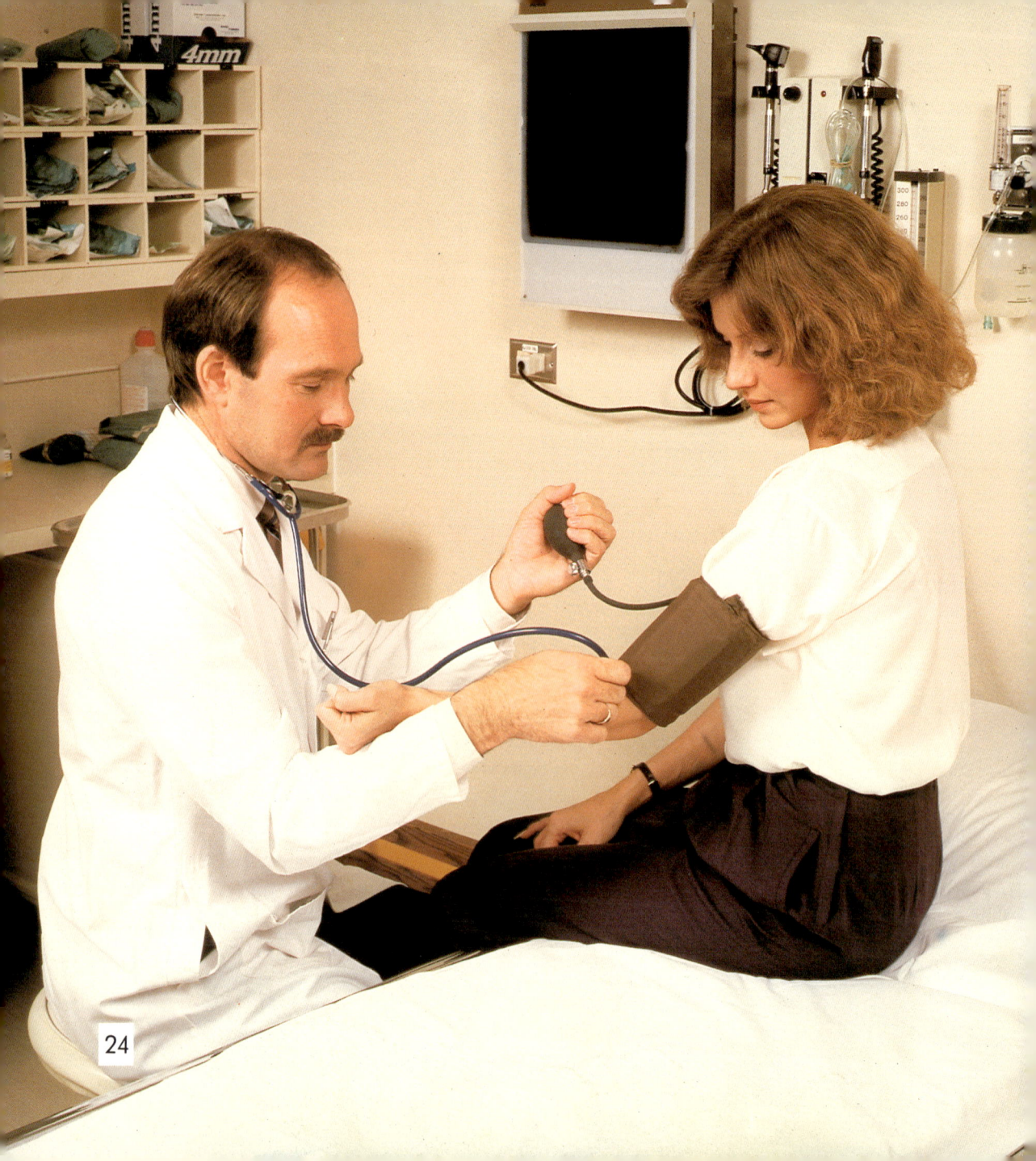

Your blood

Blood runs through every part of your body.   Your blood can tell the doctors how well you are.

The nurses take your blood pressure, and a small sample of blood. The blood is tested in the laboratory.

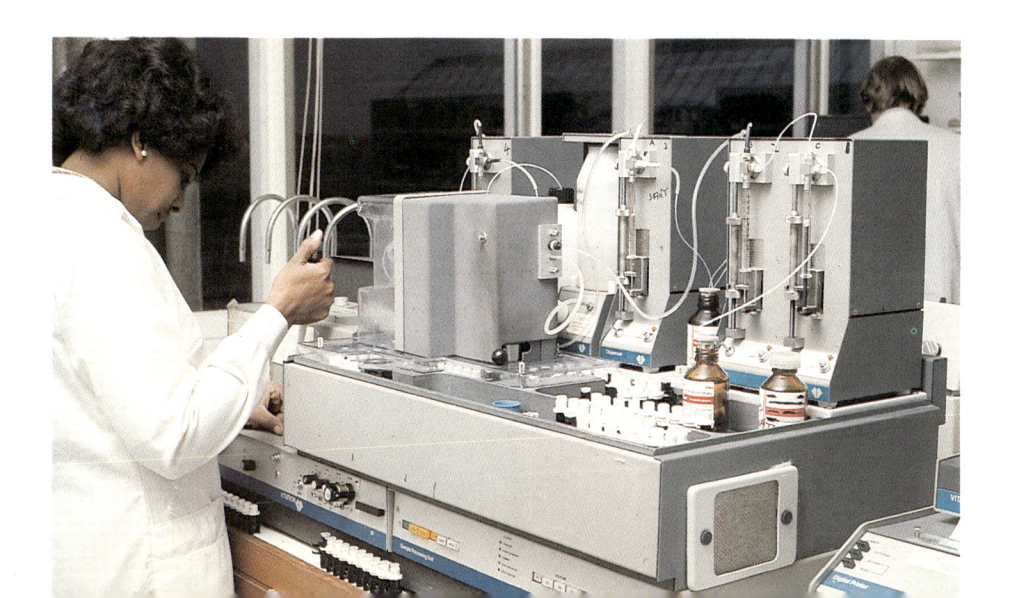

Having an operation

You may need an operation, such as having your tonsils out.   The nurses give you medicine that makes you sleep through the operation.

When you wake up you will feel strange at first, but after a while you will feel much better.

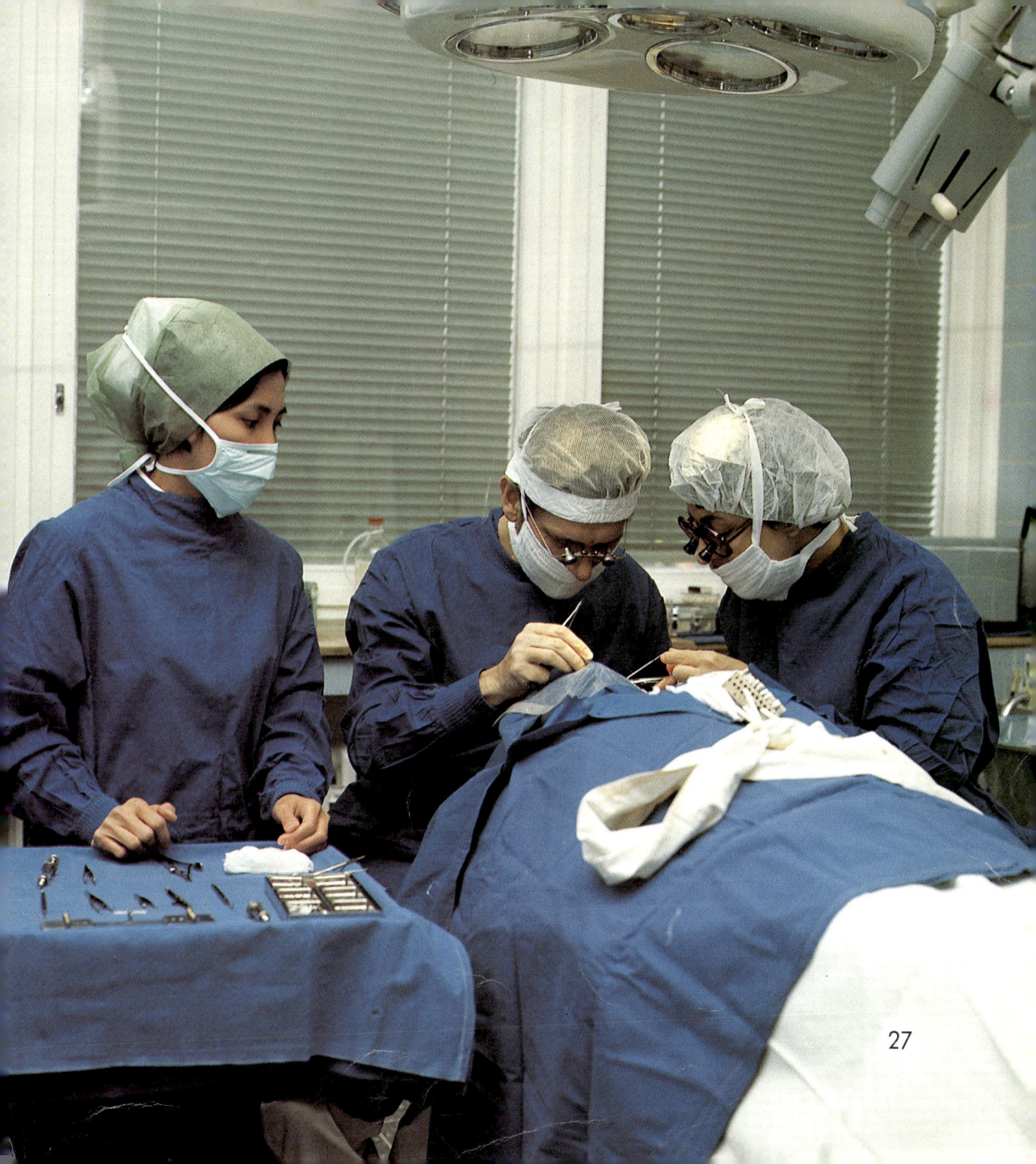

Going home

Hospital is the best place to be if you are very ill.   Nurses and doctors are there to help you and make you better.

When you are well again, you can go home.   Do you think you would ever want to go back?

29

Index

accident 11

blood 25

blood pressure 25

blood sample 25

body 20, 25

bones 8, 23

chart 16

clinic 8

doctors 8, 11, 14, 16, 19, 23, 25, 28

ears 8

eyes 8

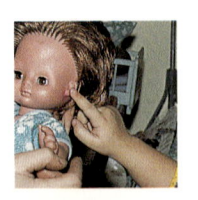